SCHIRMER'S LIBRARY
OF MUSICAL CLASSICS

Vol. 1913

Antonin Dvořák

Op. 75

Four Romantic Pieces

For Violin and Piano

Violin part edited by
Rok Klopčič

G. SCHIRMER, Inc.

DISTRIBUTED BY
HAL•LEONARD®
CORPORATION
7777 W. BLUEMOUND RD. P.O. BOX 13819 MILWAUKEE, WI 53213

Preface

Antonin Dvořák (1841 - 1904) completed his Romantic Pieces, Op. 75, for violin and piano on January 25, 1887. Two publications were used as the basis for this edition: the first edition published by Simrock in 1887, and the edition from the series *Kritické vydání podle skladatelova rukopisu* (critical edition after the composer's manuscript) published by the Antonin Dvořák Society in 1956 in Prague.

The composer himself probably supervised the Simrock edition. Therefore the violin and piano part in the piano score of this edition is the original Simrock. But, some changes have been necessary:

1. Two corrections in the Dvořák manuscript at the National Museum in Prague were made:

   a. In No. 2, m 75, the last note in the piano right hand was printed by Simrock as f2

   b. In No. 4, m 25, the third note in the violin part in the piano score was printed by Simrock as g2.

2. Editorial additions in the piano score are in brackets.

3. The last measure of No. 4 is printed as in the Dvořák manuscript. In the Simrock edition the rhythm is printed wrongly as **o.**

The separate violin part is the present editor's version.

It might be of interest to know that Dvořák wrote four compositions for two violins and viola under the titles: 1. *Cavatina*-Moderato 2. *Capriccio*-Poco allegro 3. *Romanza*-Allegro 4. *Elegia*-Larghetto. Not being satisfied with them he rewrote the set for violin and piano and called it *Romantic Pieces*. The version for strings was practically forgotten until 1945 when it was published by Hudební matice in Prague under the title *Miniatures* (Drobnosti), Op. 75A.

R.K.

Four Romantic Pieces

for
Violin and Piano

Violin part
Edited by Rok Klopčič

Antonín Dvořák
Op. 75

1

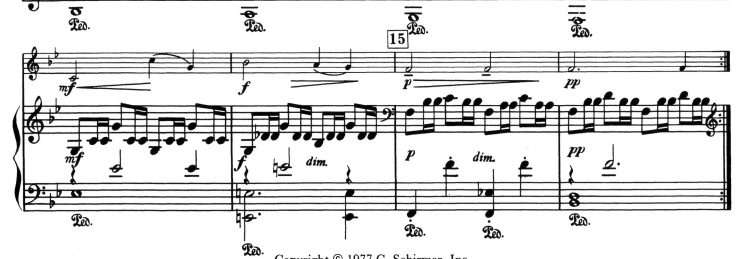

Poco meno mosso

2

Allegro maestoso

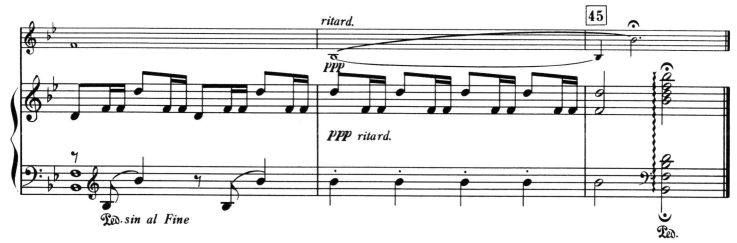

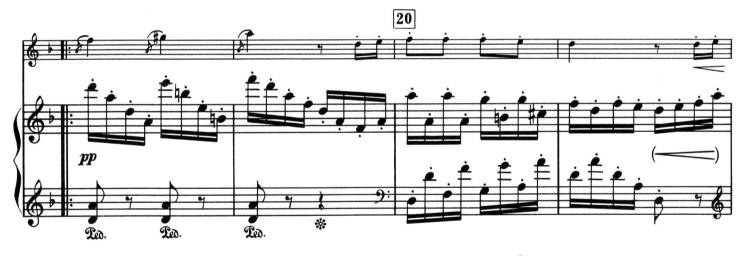

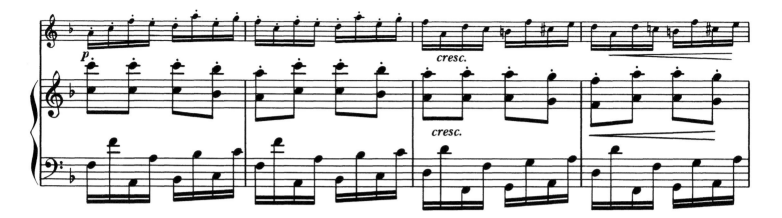

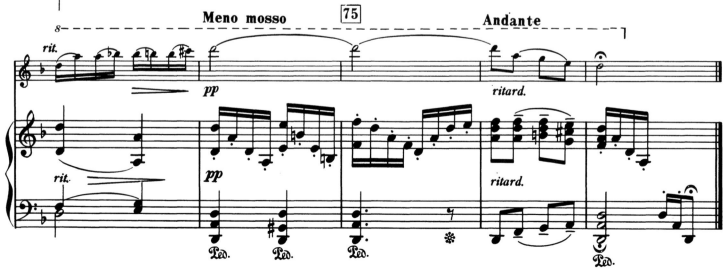

Violin

SCHIRMER'S LIBRARY
OF MUSICAL CLASSICS

Vol. 1913

ANTONIN DVOŘÁK

Op. 75

Four Romantic Pieces

For Violin and Piano

Violin part edited by
Rok Klopčič

G. SCHIRMER, Inc.

DISTRIBUTED BY

HAL•LEONARD®
CORPORATION
7777 W. BLUEMOUND RD. P.O. BOX 13819 MILWAUKEE, WI 53213

Four Romantic Pieces

for
Violin and Piano

1

Violin part
Edited by Rok Klopčič

Antonín Dvořák
Op. 75

Violin

2

3

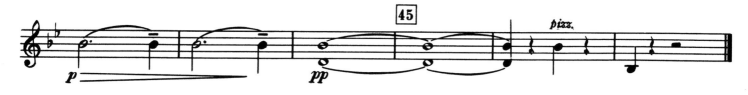

4

Larghetto

molto espressivo

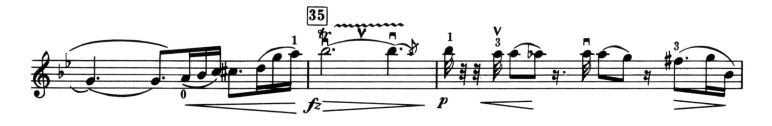

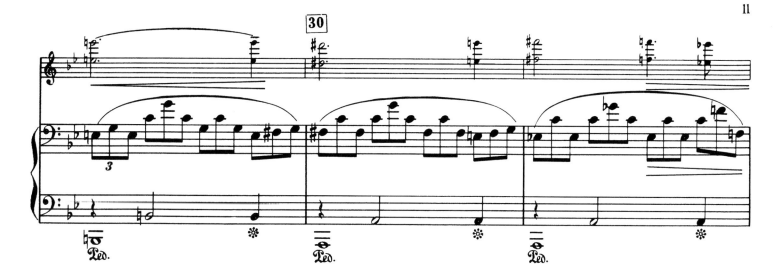

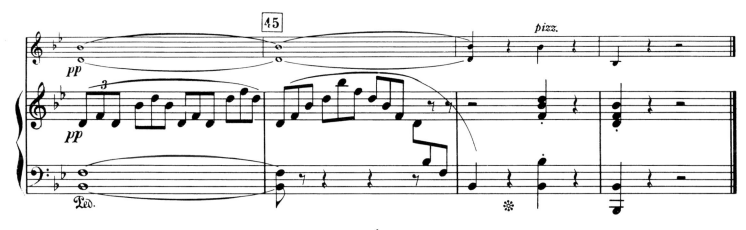

4

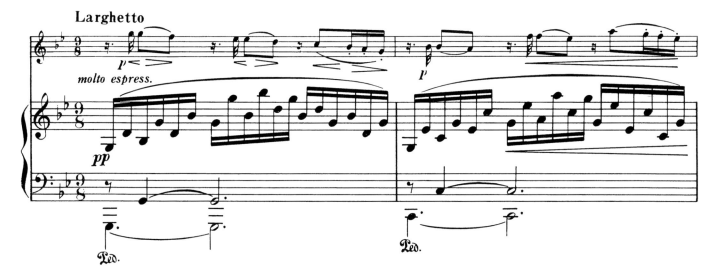

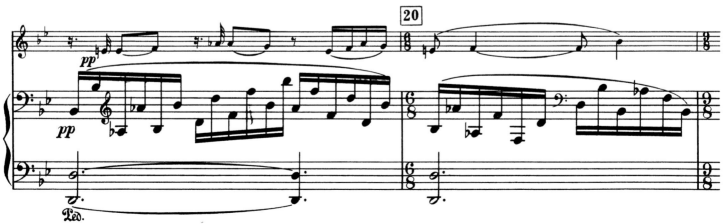

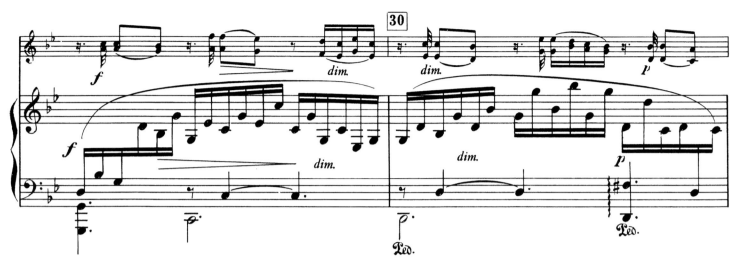